No. 1   Ozark Quilting Bee *watercolor by Frances Currey Brown ("Grandma Fran"), 1985.*

This project is supported in part by a grant from the National Endowment for the Arts.

STITCHES IN TIME
A LEGACY OF OZARK QUILTS

ROGERS HISTORICAL MUSEUM   ROGERS, ARKANSAS   1986

Library of Congress Catalog Card No. 86-60604
ISBN 0-9616640-1-0 (Hard)
ISBN 0-9616640-0-2 (Paper)

Manufactured in the United States of America

Catalog Designer: Joyce Smalley
Catalog Photographer: Larry Pennington
Peerless Photography
Catalog Printer: Conway Printing Co.

Cover Quilt loan by Kathleen Wilson
Photo by Rick Green

Illustrations are from collections of the
Rogers Historical Museum unless otherwise noted.

Illustration Nos. 3 & 4 — From Special Collections,
University of Central Arkansas, Conway, Arkansas

Illustration No. 5 — From Philadelphia Museum of Art:
George W. Elkins Collection

Photograph No. 49 — From collection of
Siloam Springs Museum, Siloam Springs, Arkansas

Photograph No. 62 — Taken by David Lewis

Photographs of Quiltmakers from Private Collections

Rogers Historical Museum
322 S. Second St.
Rogers, AR 72756

To everyone who has been comforted by a quilt or a quiltmaker

Foreword

"It is a country lending itself readily to romantic interpretation. It has rolling hills, deep valleys, jagged bluffs, rich foliage and clear streams. Set in the background, the log cabin and the rough board house, decked out with the yellow rose and the hollyhock, have an idyllic quality that is persuasive enough to make one believe that here the modern world has failed to put its restless stamp."

Indeed, as Thomas Hart Benton suggests, inveterate hill life has long eschewed the stamp of the modern world. Ozarkian people prefer to savor the prosaic—the scent of a yellow rose, hickory smoke escaping from a cabin chimney, warm apple pie, the thump of a loom, the whir of a spinning wheel, the song of a two-man saw, pink hollyhocks against a weathered log wall, the simple beauty of a calico quilt. Tradition is cherished, and the womenfolk, celebrated here, were largely responsible for handing on garden seeds, family recipes, quilting expertise and the like—mother to daughter, aunt to niece, neighbor to neighbor, bonding generations and ways of life. Many Ozarkian domestic traditions are founded in cultural patterns common to the western world. But particularization makes patterns real, and *Stitches in Time: A Legacy of Ozark Quilts* listens to the rural lisp of a universal language.

Whether dress and furnishing fabrics were handmade or purchased, few or many, the housewife has long been the arbiter of taste and the voice of authority in display and preservation. Curtains, carpets, and coverlids speak of her efforts to delight the eye, whether through high-style London silks and wools bought in eighteenth-century Boston or cottons processed at home in nineteenth-century Arkansas. The quantity and quality of the household textile inventory was a sure measure of a housewife's success; "n'airy a quilt" was an epithet no Ozark woman would want. Caroline Kirkland wrote of pioneer poverty in a log cabin with "no well-stored dresser, no snug curtains, no shining tins, no gorgeous piecework bed-quilts" and recognized the universality of quilts, "that invaluable resource in the woods." As a pelisse the quilt enveloped a shivering pioneer combatting the ague; piled with others it welcomed the visitor too late to squeeze into congested beds; hung at a window or suspended from a rafter it provided privacy in a one-room cabin.

But the quilt was primarily the summit layer of a billowy bed, and the bed—with its ample textile furnishings—is a female form of furniture. Early wills narrate the female line of descent of bedspreads and trappings, also important in the dowry. Catherine Banker writes that "A good mountain mother begins to make [quilts] for her children when they are tiny—she hopes, as each daughter marries, to be able to give her ten or twelve quilts, a feather bed, and two pillows." While the Boston bride of 1780 welcomed the gift of a mahogany bedstead hung with fifty-plus yards of watered yellow wool and a matching coverlid, the young Ozark wife rejoiced at a hickory bedstead and twelve or thirteen quilts.

In rural American homes, since the seventeenth century, beds have often been in full display downstairs, visible from the entry and the most prominent feature in the room. Frederick Law Olmsted described one Southern log cabin of the 1850s as "but a single room, about twenty feet by sixteen. Of this space one quarter was occupied by a bed—a great four-poster, with the curtains open, made up in the French style, with a strong furniture-calico day-coverlid. A smaller camp bed stood beside it. These two articles of furniture nearly filled the house on one side the door." Perhaps the conspicuous bed personified the housewife and her indisputable domain. In any case it provided an ample surface for displaying her quilts. In this the housewife was meticulous, bringing out the best Wild Goose Chase of 6,200 tiny pieces for special occasions, allotting the four- and nine-patch quilts to the ordinary.

Pride in needlework accomplishments and female self-esteem are closely interwoven in the fabric of women's history. This pride is exhibited in the topmost quilt on corded, cornhusked and feather-filled beds, in early American portraits of women with needle in hand, in late nineteenth century photographs with eye-catching quilts as background, and at Ozark picnics where women hang quilts between the trees while menfolk show off their livestock.

The demands of cloth and clothing on the frontier housewife are evident not only in boldly displayed quilts but also in the processing equipment—spinning wheels, looms, and quilting frames—that further depleted cabin space. The more provincial a housewife's situation, the greater her involvement in textile processes. "I've follered it from the field to the loom," allowed Josie Labrash of Dent County, Missouri. In many parts of America quilting frames were set up for use, then dismantled; Ozark cabins often boasted quilting frames hung from the ceiling, stored upraised but always ready for use. According to Daisy Pat Stockwell, "Women go into the room where the quilt is hanging from hooks in the ceiling; the quilt is let down in the quilting frames, a ready thimble and needle are brought from the pocket in the visitor's apron, and the women draw up their chairs beside the quilt. Soon their needles are busy as they chuckle and chat over the patchwork quilt."

Quilt tops were pieced throughout the year—in strawberry and sweet new pea season, in corn-on-the-cob days, in persimmon and pumpkin pie time, but especially in the months of beans and salt pork. After the strenuous autumn work of pickling, carding, spinning, weaving, and soapmaking, the cabin kitchen became a seamstress shop. Cushioned rocking chair before sassafras fire, kerosene lamp, buckbrush basket, protean table, Seth Thomas clock, white-curtained window, muted rag rugs, quilt-filled trunks, splint and cowhide-bottomed chairs, big blue pitcher, brownstone beanpot, and color-splashed bed set the scene. The housewife might purchase some fabrics from a mail-order house, but many more, said Harriet Beecher Stowe, were "pieces of the gowns of all her grandmothers, aunts, cousins, and female relatives for years back." The associational value of these fragments made the quilt biographical, as effective as a portrait in conjuring the image of a loved one.

Word-of-mouth invitations summoned the sisterhood for actual quilting. Sprightly, productive quilting parties rejuvenated the lonely women in the silent country: lively gossip was as bracing as spring tonic. "One might have learned in that instructive assembly how best to keep moths out of blankets, how to make fritters of Indian corn undistinguishable from oysters, how to bring up babies by hand, how to mend a cracked teapot, how to take out grease from brocade," said Stowe. Most of all one learned the details of other women's lives.

Housekeeper, gardener, field hand, nurse, doctor, seamstress, wife, mother, teacher, cook, and dairy maid, the frontier wife had a demanding life, at once relentlessly repetitive and disturbingly unpredictable. Loved ones moved away or died without rhyme or reason; life's sentence was inscrutable. The quilt allowed a woman the chance to assemble a lifetime of observation and experience in a tightly organized, sharp-edged arrangement, soul-satisfying in its clear-cut precision and logical predictability. The Ozark housewife would understand what Ellen Spaulding Reed wrote, on March 19, 1856, of "piecing me a comfortable." For the quilt was—visually, physically, and emotionally—just that.

Elisabeth Donaghy Garrett
Assistant to the Editor
The Magazine Antiques

References

Quotations in the foreword are: Thomas Hart Benton quoted in *An Ozark Anthology*, ed. Vance Randolph (Caldwell, Idaho, 1940), 59; Caroline M. Kirland, *A New Home or Life in the Clearings*, ed. John Nerber (1839; New York, 1953), 66, 210; Catherine S. Banker, *Yesterday Today: Life in the Ozarks* (Caldwell, 1941), 66; Frederick Law Olmsted, *The Cotton Kingdom*, ed. Arthur M. Schlesinger (New York, 1953), 280-81; Josie Labrash quoted in Lennis L. Broadfoot, *Pioneers of the Ozarks* (Caldwell, 1944), 76; Daisy Pat Stockwell, *Land of the Oldest Hills* (Caldwell, 1957), 24; Harriet Beecher Stow, *The Minister's Wooing* (New York, 1859, 1982), 678, 803; Ellen Spaulding Reed quoted in Linda Otto Lipsett, *Remember Me: Women and Their Friendship Quilts* (San Francisco, 1985), 81.

Preface

Quilts . . . the word evokes many different responses. For some it brings fond recollections of a kindly grandmother, mother, or aunt who worked tirelessly to provide comfort and color for a small child's bed. For quiltmakers the word registers memories of endless stitching in the act of creating. For some former teenagers it evokes guilt at having rejected the fruits of a loved one's labor in favor of store-bought bed coverings. Still others feel sorry for having worn handstitched quilts to shreds before changing views of women's work elevated these homely comforts to works of art.

But quilts are good for more than bed coverings, more than sentiment, even more than art. Quilts are valuable historical documents in which we can read a part of the past—in particular, a part that has often been neglected. It seems to me that this part addresses women's work heretofore silent and unrecognized.

Stitches in Time: A Legacy of Ozark Quilts began years ago in the depths of my own historical computer. Having grown up in the Firelands area of northern Ohio, I was quick to note the announcement of an exhibit in the Spring/Summer issue of *The Clarion*, published by the Museum of American Folk Art. *Quilts and Carousels: Folk Art in the Firelands* would open May 1, 1983, at the Firelands Association for the Visual Arts in Oberlin. Unable to attend, I sent my cousin Karen Geduldig in my stead and quickly ordered the exhibit catalog.

Soon I was reading with fascination the history of the area with which I should have been most familiar. I could not believe that so much of it was new to me. I had studied Ohio history—how had I missed so much? Then lightning struck: the earlier, 1950s-inspired history had left out the story of *her*. The addition of that story changed my heritage.

My own enlightenment made it natural for me to hope that the approaching Arkansas Sesquicentennial might awaken the people of Arkansas to their heritage through the efforts of *their* foremothers. With the encouragement of my friend Cynthia Elyce Rubin, I decided that the Rogers Historical Museum's sesquicentennial project would expose quilt history and women's history in a region of Arkansas known as the Ozarks. I found immediate interest in developing such a project into reality and was readily able to form an advisory committee of quiltmakers and other interested individuals.

Together we embarked upon what initially was called "Historical Ozark Quilts and Quiltmakers" by scheduling a "quilt sharing" in each of the five counties (Benton, Boone, Carroll, Madison, and Washington) defined by folklorist Vance Randolph as the Ozarks. Newton County residents soon reminded us that nowhere else are the Ozarks quite as prevalent as there, and we added that county to the list. In all, six quilt sharings exposed 264 quilts to our photographer, Jim Mahoney, and to our thirty volunteer researchers. After hours of interviews with hundreds of eager-to-share quilt-owners, thirty of these handmade historical documents were chosen, for their historical association with the Ozarks, for their state of preservation, and for their artistic appeal, to be included in the exhibition and catalog.

Many individuals and groups have contributed to this project. The National Endowment for the Arts, the Arkansas Endowment for the Humanities, the Arkansas Arts Council, the American Association for State and Local History, the National Endowment for the Humanities, the Charles Ulrick and Josephine Bay Foundation, the Rogers United Fund, Patchwork Emporium, and the Wal-Mart Foundation provided financial support.

Members of the project advisory committee—Carrie Wright, Nora Cope, Beth Stafford, Julie McGinnis, Patsy Vaughn, Georgia Williams, Karen Griffith, Anne Courtemanche-Ellis, Ruby Presley, Doris Briley, Mabel Obenchain, Ann Roberts, and Marthelle Harmon—gave of their time and talents overwhelmingly to organize the quilt sharings, recruit volunteer researchers, and help with the exhibit and symposium.

Folk art specialist Cynthia Elyce Rubin and Arkansas Arts Council folklorist Steve Poyser were unfailing in their good advice. Hats off as well to exhibit design consultant Virginia Westbrook, catalog designer Joyce Salley, catalog photographer Larry Pennington, and copy-editor E. B. Green. The museum's secretary, Arva Goodwin, always delivered and never complained, even under the most pressing deadlines.

Finally, personally, I thank my family, especially my husband Carl for his constant support and encouragement during the two and one-half years I have worked on this project, my daughter Brooke for her caring ways and constant smile, and my sons Blair and Brent for loving me when that was enough.

Marianne Woods
Director, Rogers Historical Museum

peculiar and exclusive province of men."

At the White River, Schoolcraft's party stayed with the Wells family, only to be shocked by the daughters' buckskin frocks, "intended to combine the utility both of linen and calico." After a supper of cornbread, butter, honey, and milk, "They could talk only of bears, hunting, and the like. The rude pursuits, and the coarse enjoyments of the hunter state, were all they knew."

By the time they reached the Holt residence, Schoolcraft was more empathetic, finding the women "frequently exposed to the inclemency of the weather, always to unusual hardships and fatigues, doing in many instances the man's work, living in camps on the wet ground, without shoes, etc." Mrs. Holt hadn't lived in a cabin with a floor for several years, had frequently moved, and had had four children die before they reached the age of two. Still, the animal-based lifestyle of the hunter's families disgusted Schoolcraft. Specifically deploring the absence of gardens, he noted before departing that "no cabbages, beets, onions, potatoes, turnips, or other garden vegetables are raised." On his way back down the river, Schoolcraft was happy to meet a keelboat headed to the settlements to trade calico for bearskins.

Other changes were on the way. In January of 1819 Thomas Nuttall came up the Arkansas River to find many new settlements, and by

No. 4 *Part of the Boston Mountain Range, Newton County. Illustration from David Owen's* First Report of a Geological Reconnoissance of the Northern Counties of Arkansas, 1857-1858.

March Congress had created the new Territory of Arkansas, including what is now Oklahoma. The *Arkansas Gazette* was founded at the territorial capital, Arkansas Post. White settlers cast an increasingly covetous eye on the Boston Mountains and beyond, though the Cherokee still owned it. By 1820 roughly 14,000 people lived in the Ozark region north of the White River.

The following year many found themselves living in the new state of Missouri, and there were new cries about Arkansans prohibited from "the garden spot of the whole territory." A western boundary was imposed in 1825 on both Indians and whites, and in 1826 soldiers from Fort Gibson rode out to remove six families (named Alexander, Shannon, Simp-

son, Simpson, McGarrah, and McGarrah) from what is now Washington County. The soldiers reminded the settlers that the land belonged to the Cherokee by drawing their swords and cutting down all their corn. The McGarrahs and company simply called it an early harvest and stayed put. Earlier, Schoolcraft had noted that the McGarrahs owned clothing of foreign manufature and that their house "bore some evidence that the occupant had once resided in civilized society."

Relatives of the Shannons homesteaded that year near what would soon be Evansville. John V. Gray, born January 19, 1794, and his wife Mary G. McBride Gray, born on the same date in 1800, had three children under the age of six. The young couple had been married on

3

October 28, 1819, in Williamson County, just south of Nashville, Tennessee. Family tradition has it that they drove teams of oxen along the Arkansas River and over the Boston Mountains with four or five other families, perhaps those mentioned above. Their youngest, James Alexander Gray, died in October, but with the surviving children, George Washington and Anne Tennessee, the Grays raised a comfortable home on the rich, well-watered bottomland. Around the outside, Mary Gray, called Polly, carefully planted cuttings of moss rose from Tennessee, filling out her new garden with lilacs and peonies. The flowers still bloom in what once was the dooryard of Polly Gray's Evansville cabin, but another manifestation of her sense of beauty—her quiltmaking—interests us more.

The art of quilting, the practice of putting a thick layer between two thinner ones and sewing it all together, goes back to the Middle Ages at least. Quilts of both ultilitarian and decorative mode seem to have been quite common in England and western Europe in the fifteenth century. Limited to domestic linens and wools and a few China silks, the English achieved a variety of decorative effects through skillful embroidery stitched directly on the quilt or on pieces applied later. During the next century, the bright permanent hues in the gardenlike florals of East Indian painted cottons, newly available to the English, proved immensely popular. The Indians catered to the Elizabethan taste for centered designs on white backgrounds, and quilting designs soon reflected the cross-pollenization of Indian fabric painting and English embroidery. The chintzes became more precious as English textile manufacturers forced tariffs, so the women took up their scissors. In a technique similar to that used in applying bits of embroidery, they cut out flowers and other designs from leftover or worn chintzes and sewed them to plain grounds in the manner of "broderie perse," or "persian embroidery."

In America, where fabric of any kind was precious, only a few broderie perse cottons remain from the last quarter of the eighteenth century. Though the earliest surviving utilitarian quilts (also from the late 1700s) are of linsey-woolsey, a homespun woven fabric of linen and wool, their designs are also based on a single, central motif with parallel borders. But by the turn of the nineteenth century, American women, with their love of functional, repeatable design, were making quilts of figured

No. 5 *Although the setting for this S. J. Guy painting is unknown, Ozark quilt frames probably also doubled as children's beds in the small dwellings depicted in illustrations 3 and 4.*

and unfigured cloth, with motifs in multi-unit block construction.

Polly Gray's lovely indigo and white quilt (06), in what is usually called the Whig's Defeat pattern, reflects an early stage in the transition from single- to multi-unit design. Originally, it seems to have consisted of four blocks, each with a central medallion surrounded by a Wild Goose Chase border. The quilt is now in pieces, and the quiltmaker's great-granddaughter has framed a surviving block as a tiny eighteenth-century, single-unit quilt.

Dating this quilt is a problem. Family tradition maintains it was made in 1826; and indeed, the quilt was exhibited in a centennial celebration at Cane Hill in 1928. But how could Polly Gray have found the time, the heart, and the materials to make such an elegant quilt in the same year that she journeyed to Arkansas, established a new home, and lost her son? To further complicate matters, the pattern seems to date, as do all documented existing examples of Whig's Defeat, from the presidential elections of 1844 when Henry Clay, a Whig, was defeated by James K. Polk, a Democrat, or 1852 when Democrat Franklin Pierce whipped "Old Fuss and Feathers," Winfield Scott, forever banning the Whigs. The Gray family has always called the pattern the Arkansas Democrat, recalling that John V. was an Andrew Jackson man. Quite possibly the pattern with its rooster-tail plumes harks back to the founding of the party under "Old Hickory."

That Polly Gray was sewing in Arkansas in 1828 is verified by a sales receipt listing her purchases at Lewis Evans's store on July 28: "2 oz. indigo, 2 oz. madder, coffee, sugar, and 1½ yards of calico." What she made that time we don't know, but her skills are recalled by mementos other than the remnants of her quilt. Great-granddaughter Frances Jones points with pride to a sleeve board: "When she tailored their clothes, she pressed the sleeves with that. She passed those skills on to my grandmother, and my grandmother to my mother. They were all very excellent needle people."

By 1829, when Polly and her family were recorded in the first census by store-keeper/sheriff Lewis Evans, many "needle persons" excellent and otherwise had journeyed to northwest Arkansas. The Cherokee had finally given up in 1828, trading their Ozark holdings for land in what is now eastern Oklahoma. By treaty, the current western boundary for Arkansas was created, and the northwestern section of the new territory was designated Washington County, with its county seat near the McGarrahs' new home. The new settlement was first called Washington Courthouse, but when confusion arose over the pre-existing town of Washington in southwestern Arkansas, its name was changed to Fayetteville for Fayetteville, Tennessee, in turn named for the Revolutionary War hero Marquis de Lafayette, who toured America in 1824. Other settlements grew around Lewis Evans's store and at Cane Hill, and both towns founded Cumberland Presbyterian academies. Carroll County was created in 1833, and a settlement around the home of James Jones soon became known as Carrollton. Two years later the area was part of the new state of Arkansas, with new counties created north and east of Washington County, one named for Thomas Hart Benton, champion of western expansion, the other for former President James Madison, who died that year.

Most of Benton County's early settlements were along a road used since the Osage had traveled it alone. It was known variously as Springfield Road, Ridge Road, Old State Road, and later as Old Wire Road. Along it sprang up such towns as Garfield, Elkhorn, and Brightwater, the last established in about 1840 by Enoch Trott, who operated a campground for drovers and other travelers as well as a tavern and grocery. Trott's Stand was a favored stop for the thirsty and weary. Some rested there and moved on; others liked the place and lingered.

Among the latter was a Scotsman named Weaver and his wife Frances. Frances Weaver, born in 1806, came to this country directly from Scotland after marriage. She and her husband homesteaded somewhere between Brightwater and Garfield, roughly in the period 1829-1845. Family tradition has it that the Scotsman cleared a great stretch of timber. "They were great hands to work in the timber," says great-granddaughter Ortha Obedia Outlaw. Frances Weaver was barren, but she cared enough about having a child to travel all the way to Texas to adopt a child named Walker, who may or may not have been related to Frances or to the mapmaker David Walker. If the Weavers made the trip to Texas in 1845 when it became a state, Frances would have been thirty-nine years old.

The one solid document of the Weaver story is an Ocean Wave quilt (07) discovered in 1937 in a trunk belonging to Frances's daughter-in-law, the former Miss Grimes of Garfield, who married the Walker boy from Texas. On Mrs. Walker's death, the trunk was opened and inside were ten quilts reportedly made by Frances Weaver. Each of the ten Walker children (Weaver grandchildren, eight boys and two

No. 6   *The Democrat, made by Polly McBride Gray,*
c. 1826-1836, 31½" x 31½", owned by Frances W. Jones.

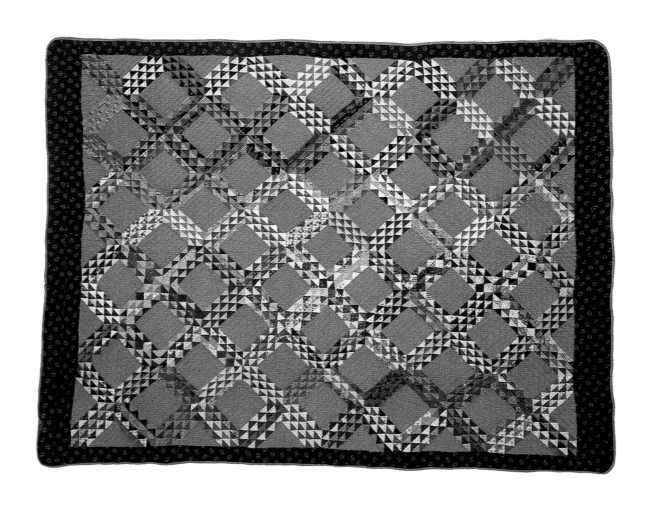

No. 7   *Ocean Wave, made by Frances Weaver, c. 1846, 67″ x 87″, owned by Ortha Obedia Outlaw.*

girls) eventually received one of the quilts, though at least one of them, Ortha Obedia Outlaw's father, wasn't born until thirteen years after Frances Weaver's death.

Nine of the quilts have disappeared, but Ortha Obedia Outlaw has cared for hers. Its Ocean Wave pattern is worked in shimmering triangles of madder and indigo and tiny calico prints. With its deep blue border and home-spun back, the quilt perfectly evokes the memory of a woman who crossed the Atlantic to settle on the Arkansas frontier. Like the arrival of the Weavers, the creation of the quilt cannot be absolutely pinpointed in time. A circa 1850 date seems reasonable; even if Frances produced the the quilt on her deathbed, it is one of the earliest published examples of this seaworthy design.

The midcentury date provides a milestone for the histories both of Arkansas and of quilt-ing. In northwest Arkansas, the frontier was all but past. Newton County had been created in 1842 out of the remote southern portion of old Carroll County, and the last of the Cherokee had come and gone on the Trail of Tears. Fayetteville had become a substantial town of 600 residents with several shops and a weekly newspaper. The town's reputation as a center of learning was firmly established with the Ozark Institute, Arkansas College, Miss James's Academy for Young Ladies, and Miss Sophie Sawyer's Female Seminary. Women, both in and out of such educational institutes, were thrilled with the new aniline dyes. Almost as quickly as the bright new colors (mauve, aliz-arin red, green, and brown) appeared, quilt-makers put them to use.

Through the new dyes and the influence of women's magazines, quiltmaking achieved a new vogue. The dyes made designs like red and green floral appliqué possible; and as early as 1851, *Godey's Magazine and Lady's Book* was telling subscribers that "as a change from the accustomed routine of knitting or crochet, the production of ornamental patchwork will be found an agreeable occupation." And in 1857 the magazine informed readers that "As the time of year is fast approaching for those happy in-door evenings with their pleasant and easy occupations which help to make home so dear, we think it requisite that we should offer a suggestion for one of those tasteful works which are of ceaseless variety in their execution, and are, when completed, worthy of becoming family heirlooms."

Not only urban sophisticates practiced the craft. George Washington Harris, local-color writer of the eastern Tennessee hill country, published a widely circulated piece called "Mrs. Yardley's Quilting," poking fun at the country women and their serious devotion to quilts. Harris's mountaineer, Sut Lovingood, ex-plained Mrs. Yardley's untimely death this way: "Her heart stop't beatin 'bout losin a nine dimunt quilt. True, she got a skeer'd hoss tu run over her, but she'd a-got over that ef a quilt hadn't been mix'd up in the catastrophy. Yu see quilts wer won ove her speshul gifts; she run strong on the bed-kiver question. Irish chain, star ove Texas, sun-flower, nine dimunt, saw teeth, checker board, an' shell quilts; blue, an' white, an' yaller an' black coverlids, an' callickercumfurts reigned triumphan' 'bout her hous'. They wer packed in drawers, layin in shelfs full, wer hung four dubbil on lines in the lof, packed in chists, piled on cheers, an' wer every-whar, even ontu the beds, an' wer changed every bed-makin.''

Evidently, Arkansas women were just as serious about quilts. Take, for example, Isabella Engels. Isabella's parents, James Kinnibrugh and Jane Moore Kinnibrugh, had come to Arkansas in 1828 and settled west of where organizers had laid out the Washington County seat. Forty years later, the area would be known as Engels's Mill and then as Farmington, but when Isabella was born in 1834, there were only a couple of isolated farms. Playmates were as scarce as neighbors in general, and, if she knew, young Isabella must have been pleased when her neighbor Abraham Allen rode off to Batesville to fetch his nine-year-old nephew.

The boy, William Henry Engels, made the long ride from Batesville to Fayetteville and into the country on the back of his uncle's horse. His mother had died in 1835 when he was only five, and he had stayed on with his father and his sister and his brother. But he was the baby, times were hard, and when someone suggested he go to his uncle in Washington County, he did. He returned to Batesville after awhile, but when his father died in 1843, he came back to his uncle, who raised him.

We don't know when William Engels first noticed Isabella Kinnibrugh, but he seems to have had long-range plans when he left his uncle in 1852 to be a wholesale merchant. As he worked like a fiend on his new occupation (even driving a herd of cattle overland to Cali-fornia), he also began work on a house near his uncle's home. After four years, in 1856, he returned to Washington County, finished the house, which is still standing 130 years later, and prepared to assume the duties of husband and father.

Isabella made preparations of her own, not

the least of which was the piecing of a quilt (08) under the tutelage of her mother. She chose for her pattern the same one Polly McBride Gray made thirty years earlier. There are differences: Polly called her quilt the Democrat and did the blocks in blue, enclosing each in a Wild Goose Chase border. Isabella called hers the Democratic Victory, used a new red fabric, and did away with borders. Mother and daughter worked hard to finish the quilt for the house William was completing. On the Engelses' wedding day, December 7, 1856, the quilt was in the frame having the last of the tiny squares worked in.

The Engels family prospered (09). The first of seven children was born in 1857, and the next year William drove a two-horse wagon to St. Louis to buy a reaper, one of the first in the county. The trip of over 700 miles and twenty-nine days was worth the effort: grain was to prove the family's fortune and protector. When a second child was born in 1860, William had already worked for some time at his uncle's gristmill, and the job exempted him from military service in 1861.

The road between Fort Smith and St. Louis brought William's reaper, but it could bring trouble, too. In February 1862 retreating Confederate troops under Maj. Gen. Sterling Price marched down the road to Fayetteville looking to replenish supplies. Trying to meet their own needs while preventing the Federals from meeting theirs led them to skim the fat, then put the town to the torch. The entire town square and many of the residences burned. Everything of value to soldiers on either side was taken or destroyed. The old White Mill, in full operation producing as much as 10,000 pounds of

No. 8 *Democratic Victory, made by Isabella Kinnibrugh Engels and Jane Moore Kinnibrugh, c. 1856, 78" x 90", owned by John Bragg.*

No. 9 *Isabella Kinnibrugh Engels and William Henry Engels in the family home.*

No. 10 *Bride's Quilt, made by Mary Jane Berthurum Stroud, c. 1870, 64″ x 80″, owned by Pat Simpson.*

No. 11 *Detail of illustration 10.*

flour a day, was unceremoniously burned to the ground.

The Engels family was spared such calamity. The mill stayed in operation throughout the war, and their fine home went unmolested. During both the Confederate raids and the later Federal occupation, they played the part of sober and necessary citizens and kept their valuables hidden. William hid his rifle in a tree; Isabella put her quilt inside the wall. After the war, Engels's Mill thrived, and the family continued to grow. Isabella took her quilt out of the wall and began new ones in earnest. Eventually she made one fine quilt for each of her seven children, including an exact replica of the Democratic Victory her mother had helped her with in 1856. The Engels family had a home, a mill, seven children, and after 1870 William laid out a town on land he owned. People had called the place Engels's Mill, but William liked "Farmington" better. Farmington it was.

About the time Engels was laying out his town, Mary Jane Berthurum Stroud was putting the finishing touches on her own creation in Pea Ridge. At thirty-two the second wife of John Wesley Stroud, she was expecting their third child. Her husband, a farmer who had come at age fourteen with his family from Manchester, Tennessee, in 1840, was ten years her senior. He had seven brothers including A. B. Stroud, whose son H. L. Stroud would become a prominent store-owner in the new city of Rogers, and a sister named America Tennessee. John Wesley's first wife had had three children before she died in the early 1860s. He took Mary Jane Berthurum as his bride sometime around 1864, two years after the Battle of Pea Ridge had destroyed many farms and families.

By 1870, things had calmed considerably, as is demonstrated in the kind of quilt (10) Mary Jane chose to make. The white-on-white elegance of a bridal quilt would have been unthinkable in the bloody days of her own wedding, but as she stitched the intricate designs into the snowy fabric she must have felt new hope for the future. Whether that hope centered on herself, her three stepchildren, her two biological children, or the child she carried, we don't know, but she gave this quilt to the son born that year when it was time for his own marriage. Her son George Stroud chose for a wife Ella Atkinson, also an excellent seamstress. Ella is remembered for the quality of her needlework and for her masterful "crazy quilts," which brought customers by train from Rogers to her home in Cave Springs. She and George proved themselves worthy of Mary Jane's optimism, keeping her work clean and white into the middle of the next century.

Such longevity is shared by the handiwork of Sarah Lucinda Coxsey Seitz (12), whose own life was brief. Sarah spent her twenty-six years in the town of Osage in southeastern Carroll County. She was born there on March 10, 1861, to John B. and Amanda Coxsey, who had come there from Tennessee. She married there on September 22, 1881, to Jesse Tucker Steele Seitz. She died there February 23, 1888, and was buried in the local cemetery.

In the six years and five months of her marriage she gave birth to five children, the youngest born just four and one-half months before her death. A photo of her in the 1880s suggests she was a delicate woman with a sense of style, and both qualities come through in another artifact, a stylish appliqué quilt (13) in the Rose

No. 12 *Sarah Lucinda Coxsey Seitz.*

of Sharon pattern. We don't know when during her marriage Sarah sewed the colorful bits of red, pink, and green cloth onto their white background or how long it took her to complete the nine squares, each containing one blossom surrounded by twelve buds and sixteen leaves. As she had averaged a new baby every eighteen months, it is amazing that she completed it at all. How could she know that she fashioned a memorial that would bloom a hundred years after her own life ended?

We know even less about the maker of a lovely Sunburst Star quilt (15) made in Green Forest, Arkansas, around 1880. The maker's

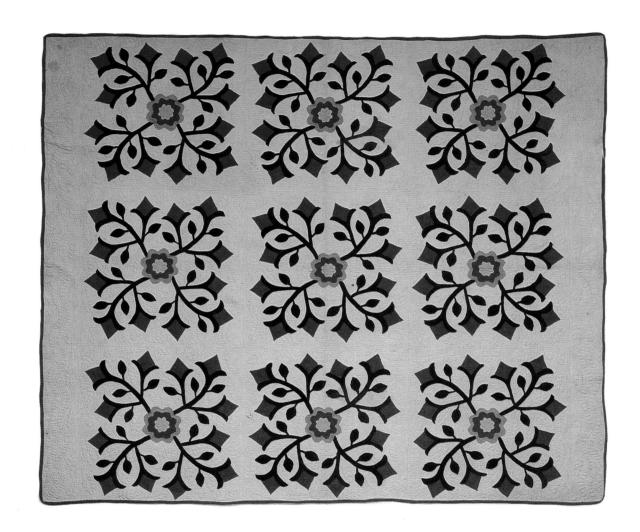

No. 13 *Rose of Sharon, made by Sarah Lucinda Coxey Seitz, c. 1885, 70" x 82", owned by Ruby Seitz.*

No. 14 *Detail of illustration 13.*

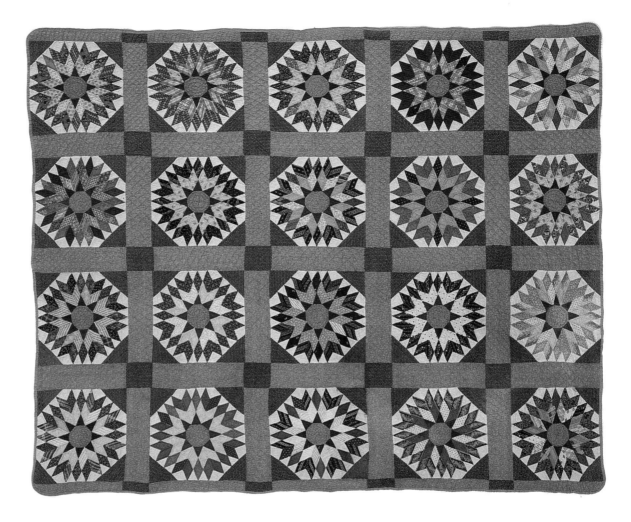

No. 15 *Sunburst Star, made by Mrs. Tharp, c. 1880, 62½″ x 75″, owned by Ova Gene Sterlin.*

No.16 *Detail of illustration 15.*

13

No. 17   *Sarah Ellen Hall Campbell, mother of four girls.*

name was Mrs. Tharp, and her daughter Nettie Woods lived her last days at the Harrison nursing home until she died in 1974. With no heirs, she chose to repay the kindness of the owners of the home by presenting them with a prized possession, her mother's quilt. In the face of such anonymity, the quilt itself must speak. Its twenty fourteen-inch blocks each contain a kaleidoscopic image in neutral colors with bright pink center. The blocks are set apart by crisscrossing bands of the same pink with green squares at the intersections. Complex geome-

tries in gray, beige, and other retiring hues contrast with simple circles, squares, and stripes of bold, eye-catching colors, drawing the eye from one to the other with no place to light. If nothing else, we know that Mrs. Tharp enjoyed the visual dance.

Time has treated Sarah Ellen Hall Campbell (17) better, though her quilt (18) has suffered. Sarah Ellen Hall was born in 1862 near Hico, which would be transformed about the time she turned eighteen into a water-cure resort town,

Siloam Springs. The boom that brought 2,000 residents in one year had tapered off considerably by 1884, when she pieced a red, green, and white quilt in the Pine Burr pattern in preparation for her marriage to farmer James K. Campbell. He had come from Kentucky with his father in 1872, had married and fathered three children before his first wife fainted, fell into the fireplace, and tragically died of the burns.

Sarah, better-known as Ellen, twenty-three at her marriage, is remembered for kindness expressed to her three stepchildren as well as to

No. 18 *Pine Burr, made by Sarah Ellen Hall Camp-*
bell, c. 1884, 79½″ x 84″, owned by Loneta Blevins.

No. 19 *Hanging Basket, made by Lydia Hudson Berry, c. 1890, 62" x 72", owned by Virginia Berry.*

the seven she bore herself. Of the latter, five were daughters, and Ellen worked a quilt for each. The eldest, Ethel Campbell, still had hers when she died in 1985, a hundred years after her parents' marriage. She remembered a mother with a bountiful heart and accurate needle as well as a father who carried her to hear Bentonville chatauquas and a William Jennings Bryan campaign speech.

Most all of the Campbells lie in Hart Cemetery now. Ellen was buried there in 1914, having succumbed at fifty-two to a bout of pneumonia on Christmas. Born in the heat of the Civil War, she died on the eve of World War I, thirty years after she had so carefully quilted her Pine Burr pattern. Today both the blood-bright reds and her attention to detail still glow, though all of the green has faded.

❦

Heavy use and frequent washing have also softened the lines of another quilt—Lydia Hudson Berry's Hanging Basket (19). Nevertheless, the image of two equal baskets chained together seems as significant today as it must have at first piecing in 1890. The Hudsons had come from Tennessee and settled on the banks of a creek just south of Old Alabam in Madison County. The creek, called Berry Branch, separated them from their neighbors, the Berrys, on the other side. The Berry family, part of a group from the state of Alabama, was responsible not only for the town of Berryville in Carroll County but also for the profusion of Alabama-related place-names in Madison County. The county itself was named for Madison County, Alabama, as was its county seat, Huntsville. It was near the community of Alabam (now Old Alabam to distinguish it from a newer Alabam just up the road) that Lydia Hudson was born in

1872, a few years after her future husband, Jonas Berry, was born on the other side of the creek.

Lydia was eighteen when she made her quilt, and if she did not think then of the joined baskets as representative of the joined bounty of the two families, she must have done so during her union with Jonas. She might have noticed later that the quilt's eight pairs of baskets, counting the split pair at top and bottom that give the illusion of rolling continuity, matched the number of children she and Jonas had. She may have used the quilt to remind the children of their double heritage, what Madison County writer Donald Harington called "bigeminality" in his novel *The Architecture of the Arkansas Ozarks.* Set in a thinly disguised Madison County, the novel chronicles generations of a family based on the Johnsons, whose descendant Virginia married Lydia and Jonas's grandson James and gave birth to another Lydia.

❦

It took more than crossing the creek to bring Missouri Ellen Gideon and William Jasper Blackburn together. William was one of six sons born to Reverend Sylvanus Blackburn and his wife Catherine in War Eagle, well north of where Berry Branch flows into War Eagle Creek. There they built a famous gristmill and fine log house that still stands more than 150 years later. William Jasper lived there from his birth in 1836 until the Civil War called him east. In Georgia he met and eventually married Missouri Ellen Gideon, and in 1869 they came home to War Eagle.

Missouri Ellen (20), born in 1842, was an asset to the community. A skilled seamstress, she made dresses for all the weddings of the

area. When her own daughter was to be married, Missouri Ellen made not only a lovely wedding dress but a beautiful second-day dress as well. Also renowned for her quilts, she prepared for the birth of a grandson by making him a quilt (21) of Princess Feather design. This pattern contains five circular clusters of eight alternating red and green feathers with two pair of extra feathers at the top and bottom. Missouri Ellen pieced it at War Eagle, carried it to Farmington, and quilted the top there, while caring for her daughter and waiting for the child to be born. The year was 1890, and the quilt and the boy turned out fine. He was given the quilt and in turn passed it on to his daughter for whom it is a treasured reminder of great-grandparents brought together by the Civil War.

No. 20 *Missouri Ellen Gideon Blackburn.*

No. 21   *Princess Feather, made by Missouri Ellen Gideon Blackburn, c. 1890, 73" x 78", owned by Ada Lee Shook.*

No. 22   *Crazy Quilt, made by Mary Elizabeth Tuttle*
Trammel, 1894, 64″ x 82″, owned by Nina Ferguson.

Nina Ferguson is likewise the proud owner of a quilt going back to the days of her great-grandparents. Her own memories reach back to the summer of 1915 when someone stepped on a nail at a church-raising, but her ties to the area go back to 1828 when her great-great-great-grandfather Solomon Tuttle drove four yoke of oxen from Tennessee over the frozen Mississippi and settled with his family near Mount Comfort, west of Fayetteville. One of Solomon's sons settled on Richland Creek east of Fayetteville, and a community known as Tuttle grew up around him. Soon he was joined there by his brother Nathan, and Nathan by his wife Ann Eliza and a daughter Mary Elizabeth.

Perhaps aware that she must get on to her destiny as the matriarch of Tuttle, Mary Elizabeth married George Singleton Trammel when she was just thirteen years old and gave birth to her first child a year later. George called her Matie, and in time she became Aunt Mate to almost everyone in Tuttle. The stream flowing near her home became Aunt Mate Branch, and at Wesley they took to calling the Masonic lodge the Aunt Mate Lodge.

Already a seasoned hand at child-raising and community relations, in 1894 she applied herself to the recent fashion for crazy quilts, making one to honor the fortieth birthday of her third child, Edward Clinton Trammel. Daughters Lula and Lizzie and neighbor Mattie Buchanon helped with a couple of the blocks, but it was Aunt Mate's quilt. Laid out in diagonal blocks, the Crazy Quilt (22) featured her skilled embroidery. Her son's birthday, her helpers' names, and some evocative little pictures of animals, flowers, and scenes were all stitched into the top. When great-granddaughter Nina Ferguson was a girl, the quilt was

her storybook, and together they pointed to the horse or the chicks swimming in the hat to tell Tuttle tales, another legacy from Aunt Mate.

No one imagined the genealogical legacy of Salona Cordelia Odom and Robert E. Lee Cornett when they married on October 14, 1893, in Dutton. The bride, born in Memphis on May 8, 1877, was the daughter of Jemima Odom and Union veteran Basil Osborn Odom. Robert E. Lee Cornett, a child of the Confederate side, was born July 23, 1867. When he was five, parents Nancy Combs and John Cornett II packed up the eight children and left their home near Hazard, Kentucky, to escape feuds and bushwhackers and make a new start. John Cornett homesteaded 160 acres in the south end of Madison County and put in a general store at Dutton. Two more children were born, but one died at age two, and the eldest daughter died, too. The youngest, Emma, was just six when her brother married Salona Odom.

Big families evidently were the rule with the Cornetts, and Robert and Salona followed suit. Nine of their ten children reached adulthood to have children and grandchildren in turn. Before they did, Salona provided each one with what she considered the necessities for starting a home. And when her tenth child Jessie married Freeman Shuster, her mother gave them exactly what she had given the others: a homemade feather bed, a bolster, two pillows, and nine quilts, including one string quilt, one nine-patch, one silk and velvet with briar stitch, one of heavy woolens, and one beautiful appliqué.

No one knows how many of the eighty-one quilts Salona made for her children still exist. Jessie has only the Pineapple Appliqué (23) stitched with ten-year-old Emma's help in

1897, sixteen years before Jessie was born. The pattern consists of four large roses or sixteen clustered pineapples, depending on what you choose to see, and Jessie considered the quilt too fine to use. A fine seamstress herself, she carried on the tradition, reproducing some of her mother's quilts as well as providing a tulip quilt for each of her thirteen grandchildren.

Mary McCollough Maxwell was born December 9, 1867, in the northeast end of where Madison County borders on Carroll. Her family had lived in the area awhile; great-grandfather Nathaniel Bunch was a charter member of the Liberty United Baptist Church organized in 1844. When Mary McCollough was nineteen, her mother died, leaving her to see after eleven younger brothers and sisters, the youngest only eighteen months old. Not until August 3, 1903, after her baby brother had turned eighteen, did she marry. Joel Maxwell, who had left Liberty to work as a cowboy, returned full of tales but ready to buy a 104-acre farm in the area. Mary McCollough, who could see he was a hard worker, had found her match.

Mary celebrated her union by piecing a quilt (25) in the French Smoothing Iron pattern. She obtained the colorful cloth by sewing for neighbors in exchange for scraps of fabric, a dear commodity even at three cents a yard. She raised her own cotton for batting in a little dooryard patch and carded it herself. Her daughter Olie Sugg recalls how, for later quilts, Mary's five children picked cotton seeds out by hand to prepare the fibers for carding. Mary McCollough Maxwell made many quilts before she died in 1946, and now Olie makes a living from the quilts and afghans she sends to customers all over the country.

No. 24 *Salona Cordelia Odom Cornett.*

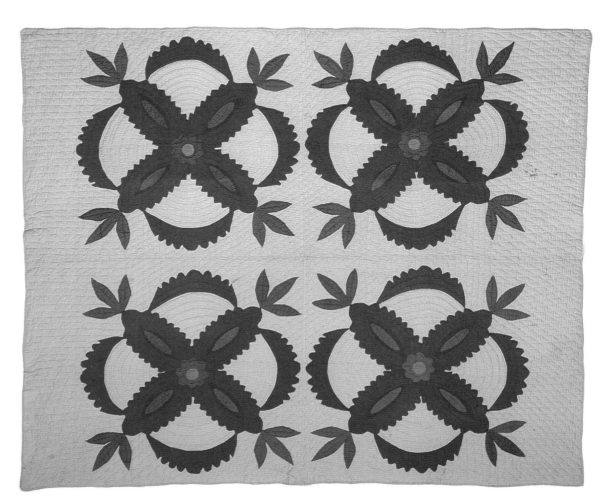

No. 23 *Pineapple Appliqué, made by Salona Cordelia Odom Cornett and Emma Cornett, c. 1897, 68" x 80", owned by Jessie Shuster.*

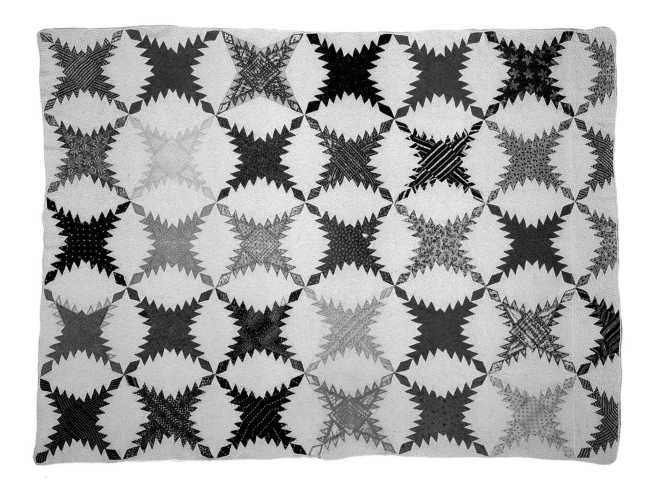

No. 25 *French Smoothing Iron, made by Mary McCollough Maxwell, c. 1903, 60″ x 78″, owned by Olie Sugg.*

Martha Boatright Ray was born just a year before Mary Maxwell, in Dryfork, less than ten miles from Liberty Church. Her parents had come to that part of Carroll County from Tennessee before the Civil War, and like Mary she lived out her life in the Kings River country. She married Thomas Ray, a farmer and merchant roughly ten years her senior, from nearby Alabam. Martha had no children, so her mother helped her piece a quilt (26) in the Rocky Mountain Road pattern the same year Mary worked on the French Smoothing Iron. Martha Ray was able to purchase her fabrics new, probably paying the same three cents a yard for her bright red cloth that Martha's neighbors paid for theirs. It is easy to wonder whether these two women, of similar time, place, and interests, might have been friends.

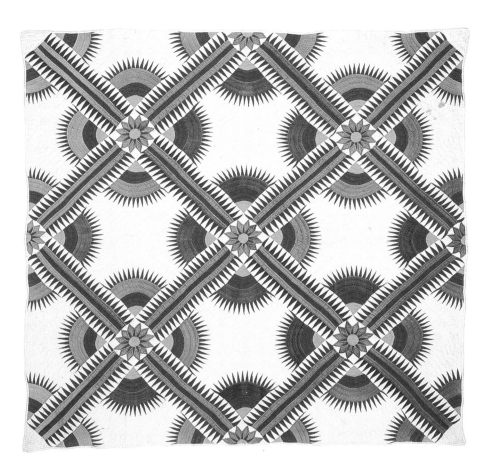

No. 26 *Rocky Mountain Road, made by Martha Boatright Ray, c. 1900, 71½″ x 73″, owned by Eleanor Counts.*

No. 27 *Detail of illustration 26.*

23

The odds are pretty good that neither Mary nor Martha ever met Gertie Davis Stinett (29). Thirty years their junior, she was born near McIlroy Gap in rural Newton County. Gertie married farmer Loe Stinett when she was a teenager, and the couple lived near Gaither in Boone County where their only son was born in 1910. Not realizing she would outlive him, Gertie decided sometime around 1914 to make a quilt (28) for him to remember her. She selected what on first glance appears to be the popular Princess Feather pattern, but which she called Wave of the Ocean.

Gertie's quilt bears no relation to the shimmering triagles Frances Weaver put together around 1850. As a nautical scene, it is one of four whirling hurricanes or a quartet of sucking whirlpools. The oaklike leaves framing the pattern are some sort of sea vegetation washed up along the quilt's shoreline. The fancy quilting worked into the muslin background brings back the feather image, forcing a search for some meeting ground between the element of water and the creatures of the air. Gertie may have intended to depict the story of Noah and his dove or the Ancient Mariner and his albatross. Whichever we choose, the quilt is a virtuoso performance, a quiet, evocative work of art.

Such musings, perhaps strange to Gertie, were everyday stuff to Nancy Ida Corbett. Born in rural southeastern Iowa in 1863, Ida Corbett was a student of the mind, and when few men and virtually no women went to college, she pursued learning through voracious reading, correspondence courses, and chatauquas. She also was a great admirer of Emerson's "Self-Reliance," a feminist, and a free thinker. After she became the third wife of George Frederick Knerr, an Allerton, Iowa hardware store manager, she made sure their four children received college degrees.

Ida Corbett Knerr's voracious reading brought the family to Arkansas. William R. Lighton's "Story of an Arkansas Farm" in the January 22, 1910, issue of the *Saturday Evening Post* chronicled his flight from the city to a small farm near Fayetteville. Reprints handed out by realtors and railroad companies and a book-length version of the story further extolled the virtues of country living. America was ready for back-to-the-farm romanticism, and Ida Knerr was one of the first to catch the fever. In the spring of 1910, the Knerrs made several trips to Arkansas in search of a place to escape the hustle and bustle of Allerton. They finally settled on a splendid two-story Georgian brick house built in 1872 by Fayetteville's Judge

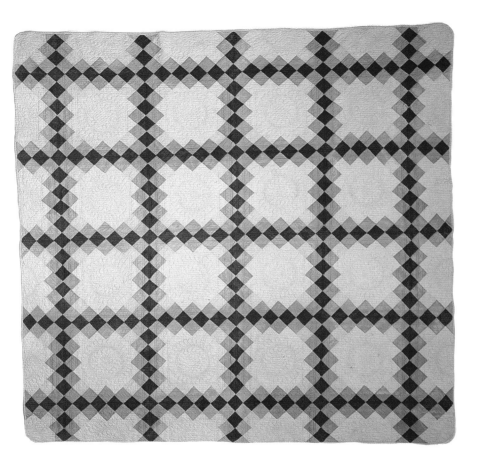

No. 30 *Double Irish Chain, made by Nancy Ida Corbett Knerr, c. 1916, 78" x 79", owned by Betty Williams.*

No. 31 *Detail of illustration 30.*

ELEVENTH ANNUAL FAIR

Washington County
Fair Association

1916

First
Premium

David Walker. The house still sits on a south-facing hill overlooking the White River Valley, not far from Lighton's Happy Hollow Farm.

By November the Knerrs were settled in their palatial farmhouse, the very picture of prewar rural enthusiasts. Fayetteville's nationally known J. H. Fields and others photographed the house in the snow with the Knerr's three daughters, as well as the whole Knerr family in rustic dress, sharpening scythes and the like. Ida Corbett Knerr tried her hand at quilting, proving herself as adept at that as at everything else she attempted. Her Double Irish Chain (30) pieced in red, gray, and white with handsomely executed quilting, won a first-place ribbon at the 1916 Washington County Fair.

Ida Knerr was an atypical woman no matter where she lived, and her prize-winning quilt was a cut above even the other fancy quilts at the county fair. Like most of the quilts in this exhibit, it was created as an heirloom, carefully stored away, never to be used. But alongside these ran a parallel tradition of vernacular, functional quilts, short on elegance but warm on long winter nights. A Scrap Patchwork quilt (32), made by Minnie Villines of Newton County between 1910 and 1920, illustrates this tradition.

Minnie Edgeman Villines, who could trace her family back to Holland by way of Tennessee, was born in 1890 close to Boxley on the Boston Mountains side, toward Deer. Her husband Hez was part of the huge Villines clan whose descendants include country singer Merle Haggard. The Villines and Edgemans were ordinary hardworking people, and Minnie made her quilts out of necessity. After a day of canning or garden work followed by cooking, serving, and cleaning up the evening meal, she would sit down to whatever handwork needed to be done. Sometimes it was a pile of cotton to be carded or dyed or spun or woven; sometimes she worked with wool from the sheep she raised. In the winter she sewed bits of cloth into serviceable tops and quilted them to plain backs with a good layer of home-grown cotton inside. Later she tried her hand at fancy quilts like the Double Wedding Ring, but none of those ever matched the simple beauty of her humble patchwork.

Such beauty would not have been lost on Mae Lewis Myers, though she came from a different world. Mae was the only survivor of the Lewis family, well known in Washington County for success in retail and banking. Her father James W. Lewis, born in Murfreesboro, Tennessee, in 1841, had moved with his widowed mother and brothers and sisters to Springfield, Missouri, in 1853. He married Jen-nie Thompson in 1868 and went to work as a wagonmaker for the Springfield Wagon Company. In 1883 they and their five children, including Mae, boarded the train for a farm at Mount Comfort west of Fayetteville. There three more children were born before the family moved into Springdale.

After the move two of Mae's sisters died, but the family prospered. James W. operated a successful wagon shop and eventually served as mayor. The oldest son Art went to work at W. T. Farrar's hardware store in 1885 and was eventually joined by his four brothers. The business was rechristened Lewis Brothers Company in 1912, and Art became president of the First National Bank of Springdale. Mae married John Holman Myers on October 25, 1891, and he opened his own Springdale Cash Dry Goods Company the following year. He served as a director of her brother's bank and president of the country club, and came to own two farms on the White River.

Mae, too, was active in community affairs, belonging not only to the Methodist church but also to the Golden Age, Chi Omega Mother's and Booklover's clubs of Springdale. With no children of her own she doted on nieces and nephews, often presenting them with pieces of crocheted or embroidered work or one of her elegant quilts. She gave her brother Ralph's daughter Mary a stylized Posey Quilt (34) with a flowered border sometime in the 1920s. Although she doesn't know when it was made, Mary remembers the quilt as part of a group Mae distributed among her brothers' children. Such gifts were common until her death in the 1950s, shortly after she had presented each of them with a small handwritten book called "Lest We Forget." They never did.

No. 32   *Scrap Patchwork, made by Minnie Edgeman Villines, c. 1920, 60½″ x 73½″, owned by Mary Phillips.*

No. 33   *Minnie Edgeman Villines.*

27

No. 34   *Posey Quilt, made by Mae Lewis Myers,*
c. 1920, 72" x 84", owned by Mary Lewis Yoe.

Neither has Elsie Allred Bland forgotten the friends, neighbors, and relatives of her hometown of Rocky Branch, now under the waters of Beaver Lake. She remembers well each member of the Help One Another Club who contributed a block to her Friendship Quilt (35) sixty years ago. She had founded the neighborhood women's club and had conceived the idea of having members work on quilt blocks at monthly meetings. To assure blocks of uniform quality, she provided high-grade muslin from Stroud's store in Rogers. She also wanted to make sure everyone, no matter how skilled or unskilled with a needle, was represented. Her mother Martha Susan Allred (36), a fine quilter, lacked the invention for an original block, so Elsie made hers as well as her mother-in-law Mary Bland's and her sister Lela Allred's. In fact, she made eight of the quilt's thirty blocks, including the one with the club's name.

In 1940, Elsie left Rocky Branch for Rogers where she started a new group, the Aim High Club. When the building of the Beaver Lake Dam forced other Rocky Branch residents to leave, some ultimately moved to the nursing home where Elsie lived in 1985. She had given the quilt to her daughter-in-law Ruth, who knew some of the people who had worked on it, but Elsie could still call the roll, just as if the Help One Another Club were meeting again.

❧

Rhoda Eunice Cummings Counts didn't have a club to help her with her quilting. She worked alone on the farm near Wesley, where she was born on October 11, 1885. Her parents, J. and Caledenia Cummings, had come to Madison County from Tennessee. Her husband Lewis Marvin Counts was born on September 2, 1878, at Wesley, not far from where his

No. 35   *Friendship Quilt, made by Elsie Allred Bland and the Help One Another Club, c. 1924, 68½" x 82", owned by Ruth Bland.*

No. 36   *Elsie Allred Bland (left) and Martha Susan Allred (right).*

29

grandfather George Washington Counts, also from Tennessee, had settled in 1829. Lewis's father had been one of twelve children. Lewis and Eunice (38) were married in 1903 and had eight children.

Eunice's first child Eugene H. was born August 3, 1904. For his marriage to Ora Wilson on September 15, 1928, she made a stunning Wheel of Mystery quilt (37). Eunice had clipped the pattern from the *Kansas City Star*, fixing the design to paper templates, and she used bright red cloth against plain white to create a vivid optical illusion. Rounded triangles set in squares create large interlocking circles that appear and then vanish. Eunice herself appeared for the last time on January 21, 1971, after which she was buried beside her husband in the Wesley Cemetery.

Cora Ellen Hoag, maker of the lovely Lone Star Variation (39) was born in Henryville, Indiana, on June 8, 1871. She was of German extraction as was Charles Keeler, whom she married in Labette County, Kansas, in 1891. The Keelers' daughter Lena Mae was born in Oolagah in the Indian Territory, before they settled in Gravette, Arkansas. There Charles worked as a rural mail carrier and got his picture in the Fort Smith newspaper for bringing the most people to the annual Gravette Picnic. He did it by picking up all the women along his mail route in a hay wagon that day.

Around 1920 the Keelers moved into Bentonville, where Cora Ellen joined the Handicraft Home Demonstration Club and became quite active in the Benton County Fair. Keeler family attendance at the fair was mandatory, and Cora Ellen worked all year long on items for exhibition — both at her home on South-

No. 37   *Wheel of Mystery, made by Rhoda Eunice Cummings Counts, c. 1927, 64" x 78", owned by Lora Counts.*

No. 38.   *Lewis Marvin and Eunice Counts with baby Leta, 1921.*

No. 40   *Cora Ellen Hoag Keeler.*

west A Street and at meetings of the club. Around 1930, she pieced a quilt with a large burst of pink, green, and white surrounded by appliquéd yo-yo flowers and a green swag border that brought her a blue ribbon at the fair. Although she did all the work herself, Cora Ellen proudly identified herself as a member of the Handicraft Home Demonstration Club. And she remained an active member until her death in 1943.

Katherine McFadden Bell (41) put her energies into the First Presbyterian Church of Fayetteville and her son's education. She and her husband decided to retire from their farm and general store in Russellville in 1918 to see their son Bunn enroll in the University of Arkansas's Peabody School, a primary and

No. 39   *Lone Star Variation, Cora Ellen Hoag Keeler, c. 1930, 81" x 84½", owned by Jo Anne Rife.*

No. 41 *Katherine McFadden Bell.*

secondary school providing practice teaching for education majors. The three Bells, along with another boy who came to attend the university, took an apartment in the old Oliver house.

Bunn finished at the Peabody School and began work at the University of Arkansas in economics and history. With World War I in progress, male students were required to drill six days a week, but Bunn was never called, and he was able to take his degree in 1923. He graduated on a Saturday and went to work in the university president's office the following Monday morning. Except for a two-year hiatus in Fort Smith in 1924 and 1925, Bunn worked the next forty-two years for the university. In 1926 he built a house near the Fayetteville park and proposed marriage to Louise Shores. They were married in 1927, and Bunn installed his bride and widowed mother in the new house.

They made a happy threesome. Bunn enjoyed his work at the university and with the Boy Scouts, and Louise became the first married woman with a living husband to teach in the Fayetteville Public Schools. Sometimes Louise and Bunn fussed that Katherine worked too hard on housework and special projects, and they were concerned when she went off to Campbell-Bell's Department Store and bought fabric for a Tulip Quilt (42). They cautioned her for nearly a year as she appliquéd the top, lined it with unbleached muslin, and quilted the whole thing herself. But as she prepared to finish, they became proud of her work and encouraged her to sign and date it. She refused to sign the quilt, but she did stitch the date she completed the quilting in one of the corners: October 13, 1930. Katherine lived fifteen years longer, making sure the quilt was used rarely if at all. Bunn and Louise know better than to invoke the ire of a conservative Presbyterian even after she's gone, and they keep the quilt put away, too.

Jimmie Glee Vaughn likes to keep her mother's quilt (43) where company can see it. Jimmie was born under that very quilt in 1938, three years after Jim Vaughn and Dorothy Luallen were married in Boxley. Like Minnie Villines, Dorothy Luallen had been born an Edgeman, in 1910. In Boxley, her father ran a general store that sold feed in colorful hundred-pound sacks, which her mother made into clothing and quilts. Dorothy was twenty when she pieced her own Cottage Tulip quilt with the lavender back. She also used lavender on the front, in the spaces between the circles of flowers. Like her mother, Dorothy usually made mostly heavy quilts out of coarse fabrics like denim. Three or four of them piled on a bed guaranteed that a sleeper wouldn't roll around much. These heavy covers were called "britches quilts," and the lighter fancy ones, "shirttail quilts." The former were for warmth, the latter for show, and Jimmie Glee proudly displays her show quilt to everyone.

Like Jimmie Glee Vaughn's mother, most of the Ozark quilters were of English, Irish, Scottish, or German extraction. But other ethnic groups are represented, too. Afro-Americans came into the region as slaves of the earliest settlers, usually to the relative flat areas of Washington and Benton counties, where large-scale agriculture was possible. After the Civil War and before the widespread racism of the early twentieth century, black communities grew up in every county of the Ozarks.

No. 42   *Tulip Quilt, made by Katherine McFadden Bell, October 13, 1930, 68" x 80", owned by Bunn Bell.*

No. 43 *Cottage Tulip, made by Dorothy Luallen Vaughn, c. 1930, 59½″ x 74″, owned by Jimmie Glee Vaughn.*

The Modern Priscilla

Fall Fashion Number

OCTOBER 1909   THE PRISCILLA PUBLISHING COMPANY, BOSTON, MASS.   TEN CENTS

No. 44 *This fashion and needlework magazine provided club memberships for women throughout the United States.*

Of all these black communities, virtually the only survivor and the one most attractive is Fayetteville's Tin Cup. The nearby university provided opportunity for employment and an easy and tolerant atmosphere, probably a factor in Labe and Ballie Joiner's decision to bring their six-year-old daughter Ruth from Coal Hill to Fayetteville in 1913. Ballie found work as a maid at the Boston Store, Labe signed on with the Frisco Railroad, and the Joiners soon found themselves surrounded by new friends and neighbors.

Ruth married Olaff Carr in 1925, and they had four daughters and one son. Sometime around 1930 she and other women of the community formed a club known as The Modern Priscillas (44). Ruth and her mother were both among the members who gathered every Friday to talk, sew, and get away from husbands and dishes. The tight circle rarely numbered more than a dozen members who rotated meetings from one home to another. The Modern Priscillas were not a quilting club per se, but quilting was well suited to its purposes. The work was communal, the outcome lovely and serviceable. The club owned a frame and a pair of sawhorses to set it on, and each week the quilt in progress was carried to the meeting. With minutes and dues, The Modern Priscillas were not unlike other "ladies of the club" in America.

In other parts of the South, Afro-American quilters made quilts reflecting the textile traditions of west Africa, but in the Ozarks they chose to do their own versions of the popular patterns of the day. Today, Ruth Joiner Carr Rich has the only known surviving quilt (45) of The Modern Priscillas, an appliqué of butterflies similar to those seen hanging on clotheslines at roadside stands throughout the Ozarks. There is one small difference: the Priscillas' butterflies have brightly colored wings, but the bodies are black.

If the butterfly seemed well-suited to The Modern Priscillas, the slow-moving snail was

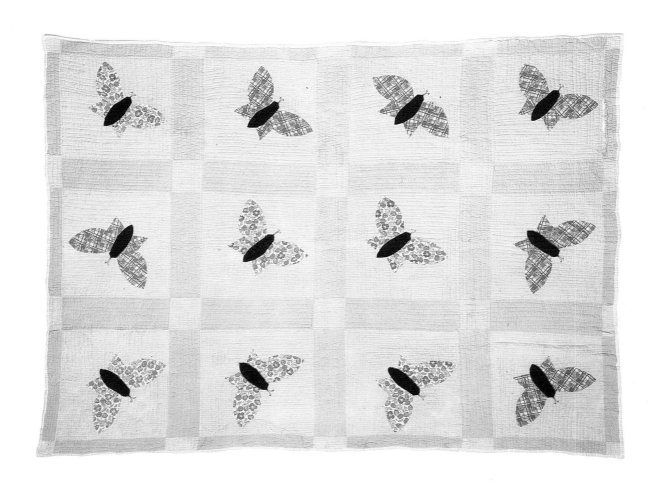

No. 45   *Butterfly Quilt, made by The Modern Pris-cillas, c. 1830, 58" x 78", owned by Ruth Rich.*

appropriate for Ida Burdick Collins, a woman much interested in the passage of time. Her granddaughter Lou Norris recalls Ida's uncanny ability to call the hour within five or ten minutes. If the clock stopped, she reset it precisely with a marked stick kept on the back porch. She began each household chore at the proper hour, and she was always very precise about how many minutes the chicken should cook on each side.

Ida was born on January 11, 1858, in Richmond, Illinois. When she was a young girl the family relocated to Kansas, where she married Wade Collins on January 10, 1876. She and Wade lived in Missouri for awhile, but the long cold winters drove them south to Arkasnas. They homesteaded forty acres of good bottomland beside Long Creek about two miles from Denver in eastern Carroll County. Their mail came by way of Alpena, but the rural route run by a Mr. Green in a horse and buggy was so long that Ida took it upon herself to care for a second horse to finish the run.

There on Long Creek, Ida and Wade raised four boys and two girls. When daughter Mina lost her husband, she came home with two children to do most of the housework and free her mother to ponder time and piece quilts. Ida made one nice quilt for each of her children, but by the time she finished she had too many grandchildren to consider supplying each of them. She did finish the Snail's Trail (46) in time for granddaughter Lou's wedding to Raymond Norris in October 1932, seven years before Ida died.

❧

Orphea Lee McFarrin Duty (48) didn't take up quilting until after her marriage. Born on

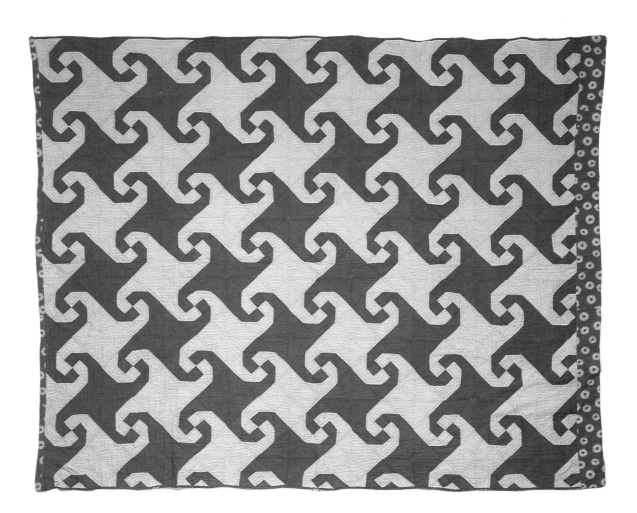

No. 46 *Snail's Trail, made by Ida Burdick Collins, c. 1932, 64" x 78", owned by Lou Norris.*

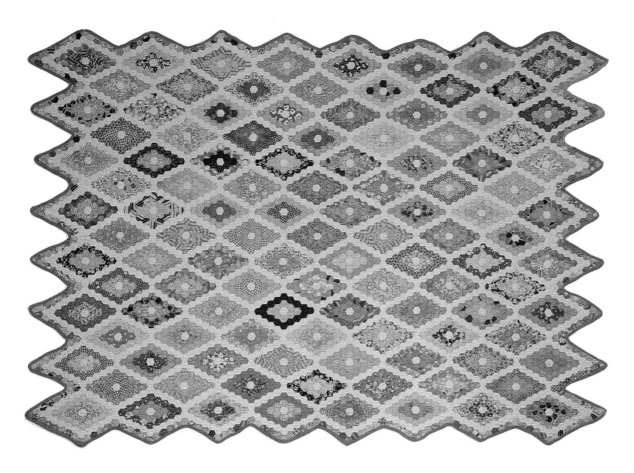

No. 47 *Diamond Field, made by Orphea Lee McFarrin Duty and Lieu Edgeman Duty, c. 1930, 66″ x 89½″, owned by Orphea Duty.*

No. 48 *Orphea Lee McFarrin Duty.*

June 12, 1898, she was seventeen when she married Fred Duty on October 30, 1915. Her own mother, Sarah Harp McFarrin, had been too busy raising five girls and a boy to have time for quiltwork. Her mother-in-law Lieu (pronounced "Lou") Duty, on the other hand, was one of the finest quilters in the county. Lieu's father was Sam Edgeman, a distant cousin of Jimmie Glee Vaughn's grandfather, who ran one of the two stores at Boxley. Orphea and her husband Fred ran the other one, the Boxley Mercantile Store. The Dutys' store carried a bit of everything — groceries, hardware, and dry goods, and when Orphea first took up quilting the store supplied all her materials.

At first Orphea's mother-in-law would only let her piece, leaving the more demanding quilting to the experts. By about 1930, however, Orphea was ready to tackle it all. She found the Diamond Field pattern in the household department of the *Daily Drover's Telegram*. As Orphea envisioned it, her quilt (47) required a larger variety of fabric than the Boxley Mercantile could offer. She sent off for three inches of yardage, enough for two blocks, of every fabric offered by both Sears Roebuck and Company and Montgomery Ward. With mother-in-law Lieu and sister-in-law Bessie looking over her shoulder and between the long hours at the store and the demands of the Home Demonstration Club, Orphea finally completed the quilt. She finished the edge with a bright pink binding, and the result was too nice for the bed or even to donate to the prettiest girl competition at the box supper. This quilt had heirloom status, worthy of both grandchildren's and mother-in-law's eyes.

Vera Drake Wade's Flower Garden (50) is on the surface quite similar to Orphea Duty's Diamond Field. Both are constructed of small groups of clustered hexagons. Like Orphea, Vera bought three inches of thirty-six-inch fabric for each two blocks. She remembers buying solid-color Peter Pan cottons from Campbell-Bell's in Fayetteville, and she got some of the florals there too. Others were gathered from different places, some by her father at little country stores while on Missouri trips to graft walnut trees. Vera relied heavily on Lura M. Jewett, who lived alone in a tourist cabin near Fayetteville's Wilson Park, to help her finish the quilt. Until Vera's husband Clifton Wade, an attorney, found a way for Lura to receive a regular relief check, Lura depended on her quilting skills for a living. She would spend long hours gently pricking a finished top with a needle to transfer a quilt design from a Mountain Mist batting wrapper without leaving pencil marks on the quilt. And after emptying several hundred-yard spools of thread, she would charge only twelve dollars. But Vera gave her twenty-five.

There were differences in the ways that Orphea and Vera worked. Orphea Duty pieced between customers at her store as Vera worked while waiting for the bus to take her from Fayetteville to teach home economics in Prairie Grove. Her route wasn't on a regular bus run; she just snagged a ride with the bus driver on his way to work and relied on traveling salesmen she knew and the kindness of chicken-truck

Phelps Photo

drivers to get home. It was the fall of 1930, Vera worked to send her husband through law school, and waiting for the bus gave her time to sew her precut hexagons together. She had come up with a unique cutting scheme, making hexagonal templates from an old blotter that adhered well to fabric. She cut out the middle of each one so that she could look through to center each floral. After that it was simply a matter of reaching into the blue or pink box for the right color. Orphea would have appreciated Vera's organization, though she would never have guessed how far Vera (51) had come.

Vera's mother Mary Shockley Drake had worked her way through Ohio Wesleyan University in a dress factory before becoming a missionary to China in 1897. Vera's father Noah Fields Drake took both master's and doctoral degrees at Stanford before leaving to teach geology and mining to Chinese college students. He was originally from Cincinnati, in western Washington County, Arkansas, where his ancestors had settled as early as 1822. Mary and Noah met and were married in China in 1904, and Vera was born in 1909. Many of her memories of childhood in China center on her

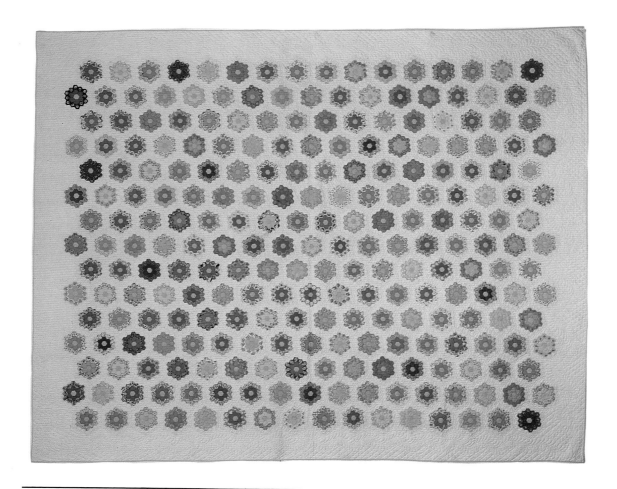

No. 50 *Flower Garden, made by Vera Drake Wade, c. 1931, 82½" x 102", owned by Vera Wade.*

No. 51 *Vera Drake Wade.*

mother, a skilled quilter who made clothing for Vera's dolls, but who died while Vera attended high school in Fayetteville. Vera's husband and friends had helped her through this loss by the time she worked on her flower garden quilt.

☙

In the 1980s, Yvonne Davis of Jasper worked for Orphea Duty's granddaughter. Yvonne, who never married, shared her home with Margaret Vann, whom she thought of as a sister, a friend of the family for over thirty years. The only one in her family interested in what she calls "relics," Yvonne has, in addition to mementos of her mother's days with the weather bureau, two quilts made by her mother's mother (a Dutch Doll and a Double Wedding Ring). She also keeps an eloquent letter from her mother's grandfather A. F. Boomer to Newton County Judge W. P. Spears in 1917, describing Pershing's march through El Paso, Texas. Yvonne has patterns for picks, shovels, and other tools made by her father and grandfather in their blacksmith shop, and she owns an elegant turn-of-the-century blouse made by her grandmother. Granny Davis also made Yvonne's treasured Seven Star quilt (52).

Lucinda Elizabeth Ann Rutledge Davis (53), Yvonne's grandmother, was born in Kentucky on November 5, 1867, to parents of French and Indian descent. No one knows when she came to Arkansas or where she married George Washington Davis. Yvonne grew up near their home in Jasper, often stopping to see her grandmother on the way home from school. She remembers that Lucinda spent all her time piecing tops, many more than she would ever see quilted. She made a Butterfly similar to that of The Modern Priscillas, cutting her butterflies by a pattern drawn on a page of the *Arkansas*

No. 52   *Seven Star, made by Lucinda Elizabeth Ann Rutledge Davis, c. 1934, 64" x 82½", owned by Yvonne Davis.*

No. 53   *Lucinda Elizabeth Ann Rutledge Davis and George Washington Davis.*

41

No. 54   *Appliqué Tulip, made by Elizabeth Gleaves Bigham and Dixie Susan Baldwin, c. 1935, 74½″ x 88½″, owned by Mrs. E. S. Bigham.*

Gazette or the *Newton County Informer*. In 1934 she made the Seven Star in a similar manner, cutting 168 stars to set inside twenty-four hexagons. When finished, she gave the top to Yvonne. It remained a top until Yvonne's neighbor Lela Briscoe quilted it in 1970, long past Lucinda's death in 1949.

Elizabeth Gleaves Bigham (55) of Berryville also values "relics." She and husband E. S. Bigham have filled their home with glass and porcelain treasures, but the house and the street are Elizabeth's main links to the past. Elizabeth's grandmother Dixie Susan Baldwin (56) was born in Booneville, Missouri, on August 2,

No. 55 *Elizabeth Gleaves Bigham.*

1862. After she and John Baldwin were married in 1878, they moved to Little Rock, where he ran a grocery store and a pecan orchard. In 1909, on their fiftieth wedding anniversary, the Baldwins retired to Berryville, and six months later their beautiful twenty-two-year-old daughter Emma Lenora Baldwin married telegraph operator Donald Lewis Gleaves from Seligman, Missouri.

The younger couple settled on Huntsville Street, where Elizabeth was born on January 11, 1912. Sometime between her high-school graduation in 1930 and her marriage in 1935, Elizabeth Gleaves joined a sewing club. Although they met largely for entertainment, Elizabeth, a girl who worked in her father's store, some women from the Berryville Drugstore, and the woman who owned the restaurant often worked on sewing projects together. Elizabeth had always done handwork, but in the club she first tried piecing a quilt. The members all started with Flower Garden tops. Elizabeth's turned out fine, so she decided to try one of the more difficult Stearns and Foster appliqué patterns. Her lavender, pink, and green Appliqué Tulip (54) worked out nicely, and her grandmother Dixie quilted it. Despite her grandmother's quilting, Elizabeth always preferred her sister Dixie's quilt to her own. The Bighams still work together every day in the hardware store her father started, and sometimes during Pioneer Days Elizabeth displays in the window an old quilt made by her great-grandmother from hand-dyed feedsacks.

Jim Miller and his parents share the Bighams' enthusiasm for antiques, and they, too, run a family hardware business. Theirs is in Harrison where Jim's father Joseph J. Miller was born in

1912, five years after his parents had married and moved there from Berryville. Joseph's father Nath Miller was the youngest of four children, and Nath's mother died at his birth. When his father died of pneumonia following smallpox, the children were sent to various foster homes, Nath to the Smiths, who already had ten children. As a young man he worked for five years in Idaho before returning to Arkansas and marrying Dora Turner (58). In Harrison, he worked first in the produce business, buying and selling chickens, eggs, green hides, dry hides, butter, and other commodities. After fifteen years, he began to raise hogs, and in 1931 he entered the hardware business.

No. 56 *Dixie Susan Baldwin.*

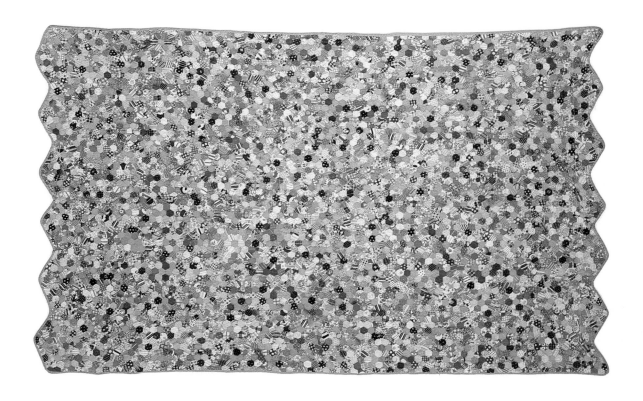

No. 57   *Honeycomb, made by Dora Miller, c. 1935,*
55" x 88½", owned by Jim Miller.

Dora was born in Berryville in 1891. Just sixteen when she married and left home for the first time, she immediately caught typhoid from drinking spring water, and all her hair fell out. But she soon rallied, and after her second son Joseph was born, she was able to take up some serious quilting on the special quilt frame her father had made in the 1890s. Unlike the typical Ozark frame that hung from the ceiling, hers sat on legs and had a crank so she could roll it up as she worked (the family's hardware store sells a modified version today). Dora's half-brother made her a quilt box the size of a sofa, and she filled it before long. One quilt won a prize at the Boone County Fair as a top one year and as a completed quilt the next.

Dora pieced and quilted all winter long, swapping patterns with friends or copying them from the *Ladies' Home Journal*. Sometimes she worked with the women of the adult Sunday school class on quilts to raise money, but mostly she worked alone. Surely that is how she completed the Honeycomb Quilt (57) in 1935. With literally thousands of tiny hexagons in an allover pattern, it is a Grandmother's Flower Garden gone wild. After she completed it, Dora Miller lived another forty years, long enough that big-city painters were making big-city dollars for paintings that looked a lot like her quilt. She probably never saw any of them, but it is interesting to think about what her reaction might have been.

✿

Mabel Clara Buell Seitz's Whig Rose (60) quilt completes the circle of this garden of quilts. Mabel (59) was the wife of Frank Massie Seitz, whose mother, Sarah Lucinda Coxsey Seitz, made the Rose of Sharon quilt we examined earlier. Mabel was the daughter of John A. and Jerusha Adams Buell, whom she lived with in Green Forest until she and Massie were married on Christmas Eve, 1902. The bride was nineteen and the groom twenty when they packed up and moved to Osage. In 1905 they returned to Green Forest.

Massie went to work in a dry goods store that belonged to his mother's family, and he was able to buy them out by 1913. Renamed Seitz Mercantile Company, the store supported the couple and their six children for fifty-six years. Mabel worked alongside her husband much of the time, but when an automobile accident in 1936 took her off her feet, she filled the time by piecing and quilting an unusual pattern of small stuffed rosebuds. She seems to have created the design herself, perhaps drawing inspiration from the Rose of Sharon her mother-in-law pieced fifty years before.

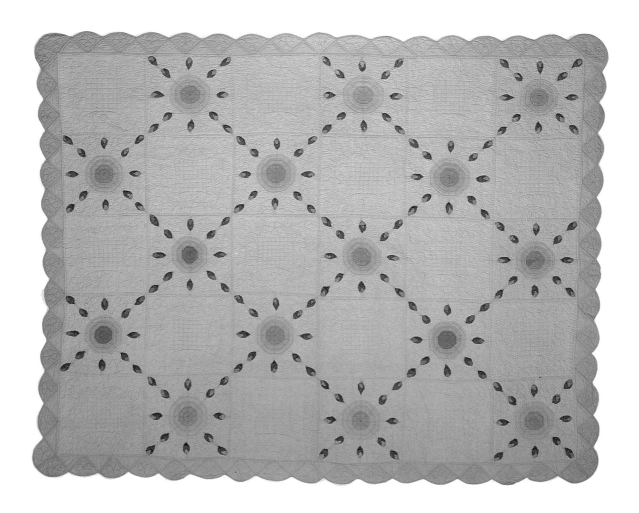

No. 60   *Whig Rose, made by Mabel Clara Buell Seitz,*
c. 1936, 75" x 92", owned by Ruby Seitz.

No. 61   *Detail of illustration 60.*

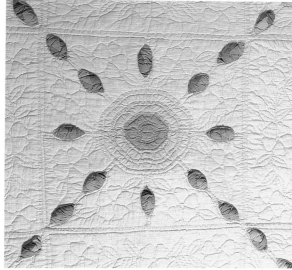

The 110 years of Ozark quilting illustrated in this exhibition (and even the nearly 300 quilts documented in the project) only begin to tell the story of the domestic art of Ozark women. Many beautiful and important quilts have deteriorated; others are locked away in closets and cedar chests; still others have left Arkansas with their makers, especially in the 1920s mass migration to California. And a great variety of tradition and innovation is found in quilts made in the fifty years since our circle was closed.

Even there the story doesn't end. Today in the Ozarks active quiltmakers, women and men, painstakingly stitch in the proven traditional ways or create designs based on old patterns and new conceptions. Both are finding new audiences and markets. Our story is only the beginning. There is still much to learn. But it is good to know that our children, too, will have much to find, in search of their mothers' gardens.❧

No. 62 *Springdale quiltmaker, Garland Cole, shows his goods to an interested customer.*

Author's Note on References

My principal sources were thirty-four tape recorded interviews conducted with the owners of quilts in the exhibit and a few of their quiltmaking neighbors. In a few cases, informants prepared written statements of the pertinent facts and anecdotes. Also helpful were the genealogies, clippings, scrapbooks, and time that these kind people shared. I hope I have related their stories as they would wish. The following sources were also useful. Quotations in the essay from Henry Schoolcraft's journal may be found in the Park edition of *Schoolcraft in the Ozarks*, information on early quilting history is from Holstein's *The Pieced Quilt*, and the Harris quotation is from Cohen and Dillingham's *Humor of the Old Southwest*.

Abbott, Shirley. *Womenfolks: Growing Up Down South*. New York: Ticknor and Fields, 1983.

"Antique Quilts Shared at Jasper." *The Newton County Times* 27 (Sept. 1984): 10.

Ashmore, Harry S. *Arkansas: A History*. New York: W. W. Norton, 1978.

Baldwin, Cinda. "A Quilting Tradition: The Centerpoint Ladies' Club." *Flashback* 31.2 (1981): 14-17, 26.

————. "Quilts, Quilters, and Quilting Practices of Northwest Arkansas: An Honors Paper." University of Arkansas, 1981.

Berry, Michael W. "Documenting the 19th-Century Quilt." *American Craft* 45.1 (1985): 23-27.

Bishop, Roberts. *Quilts, Coverlets, Rugs and Samplers*. New York: Alfred A. Knopf, 1982.

Black, J. Dickson. *History of Benton County*. Bentonville: the author, 1975.

Bolton, Charles S. et al. *Arkansas Becomes a State*. Little Rock: Center for Arkansas Studies, University of Arkansas at Little Rock, 1985.

Brown, Kent R. *Fayetteville: A Pictorial History*. Fayetteville: The North Arkansas Symphony Society, 1985.

Cohen, Hennig, and William B. Dillingham. *Humor of the Old Southwest*. Boston: Houghton Mifflin Company, 1964.

Cooper, Patricia, and Norma Bradley Buferd. *The Quilters: Women and Domestic Art, An Oral History*. Garden City: New York: Anchor Press/Doubleday, 1977.

Cornett, Essie R. *The Cornett Family*. New York: The Vantage Press, 1971.

Drew, C. Kaye. "Gertrude May Seitz — Her Arkansas Years." *The Carroll County Historical Society Quarterly*. 25.3 (1980): 13-16.

Gerlach, Russel L. *Immigrants in the Ozarks: A Study in Ethnic Geography*. Columbia: University of Missouri Press, 1976.

————, and William Wedenoja. *The Heritage of the Ozarks: A Multicultural Curriculum for Elementary Schools*. Little Rock: August House, 1984.

Glassie, Henry. *Pattern in the Material Folk Culture of the Eastern United States*. Philadelphia: The University of Pennsylvania Press, 1968.

Goodspeed's 1889 History of Benton County. Reprint. Bentonville: Benton County Historical Society, n.d.

Goodspeed's 1889 History of Washington County. Reprint. Siloam Springs: J. Roger Huff, 1978.

Haders, Phyllis. *The Main Street Pocket Guide to Quilts*. Pittstown, NJ: The Main Street Press, 1981.

Hall, Carrie A., and Rose G. Kretsinger. *The Romance of the Patchwork Quilt in America*. Caldwell, Idaho: The Caxton Printers, Ltd., 1935.

"Handicrafts and Painting." *Arkansas: A Guide to the State*. Reprint. New York: Hastings, 1958.

Harington, Donald. *The Architecture of the Arkansas Ozarks, A Novel*. Boston: Little, Brown and Company, 1975.

Hilliard, Sam Bowers. *Atlas of Antebellum Southern Agriculture*. Baton Rouge: Louisiana State University Press, 1984.

Holstein, Jonathon. *The Pieced Quilt: An American Design Tradition*. Boston: Little, Brown and Company, 1973.

Ice, Joyce. "Women's Work: Quilting in the Community Context." Paper presented at conference on Handiwork: Folklife Traditions of the South and Southwest, University of Arkansas, April 11-12, 1985.

Ickis, Marguerite. *The Standard Book of Quilt Making and Collecting.* New York: Dover Publications, 1959.

Ingenthron, Elmo. *Borderland Rebellion: A History of the Civil War on the Missouri-Arkansas Border.* Branson, Mo.: The Ozarks Mountaineer, 1980.

Kahn, Kathy. *Hillbilly Women.* New York: Avon Books, 1974.

The Kentucky Quilt Project. *Kentucky Quilts 1800-1900.* New York: Pantheon Books, 1982.

Kolodny, Annette. *The Land Before Her: Fantasy and Experience of the American Frontiers, 1630-1860.* Chapel Hill: The University of North Carolina Press, 1984.

Kunkel, Peter, and S. S. Kennard. *Spout Spring: A Black Community.* New York: Holt, Rinehart and Winston, Inc., 1971.

Lackey, Walter F. *History of Newton County, Arkansas.* Independence, Mo.: Zion Publishing Co., 1950.

McKissick Museum. *Social Fabric: South Carolina's Traditional Quilts.* The University of South Carolina: McKissick Museum, n.d.

McNeil, W. K. *The Charm is Broken: Readings in Arkansas and Missouri Folklore.* Little Rock: August House, 1984.

Morgan, Gordon. *Black Hillbillies of the Arkansas Ozarks.* Fayetteville: Department of Sociology, University of Arkansas, 1973.

Musgrave, Bonita. "A Study of the Home and Local Crafts of the Pioners of Washington County, Arkansas." Master's Thesis, University of Arkansas, 1929.

Park, Hugh, ed. *Schoolcraft in the Ozarks: Reprint of Journal of a Tour into the Interior of Missouri and Arkansas in 1818 and 1819 by Henry R. Schoolcraft.* Van Buren, Arkansas: Press-Argus Printers, 1955.

The Quilt Digest. San Francisco: Kiracofe and Kile, 1983.

The Quilt Digest 2. San Francisco: Kiracofe and Kile, n.d.

Rafferty, Milton D. *The Ozarks: Land and Life.* Norman: University of Oklahoma Press, 1980.

Randolph, Vance, and Isabel Spradley. "Quilt Names in the Ozarks." *American Speech* 8 (Feb. 1933): 33-36.

Rea, Ralph R. *Boone County and Its People.* Van Buren, Ark.: Press-Argus, 1955.

Roach, Susan. "The Kinship Quilt: An Ethnographic Semiotic Analysis of a Quilting Bee," in *Women's Folklore, Women's Culture,* edited by Rosan A. Jordan and Susan J. Kalcik. Philadelphia: University of Pennsylvania Press, 1985.

Rubin, Cynthia Elyce, ed. *Southern Folk Art.* Birmingham, Alabama: Oxmoor House, 1985.

Smith, Maggie Aldridge. *Dear Shug.* Siloam Springs, Arkansas: The author, 1976.

The Virginia Women's Cultural History Project. *"A Share of Honor": Virginia Women 1600-1945.* Richmond: The Virginia Women's Cultural History Project, 1984.

Vlach, John Michael. *The Afro-American Tradition in Decorative Arts.* Cleveland: The Cleveland Museum of Art, 1978.

Walker, Alice. *In Search of Our Mothers' Gardens: Womanist Prose.* San Diego: Harcourt Brace Jovanovich, Publishers, 1983.

Washington County Historical Society. *One Hundred Years of Fayetteville. 1828-1928 by William S. Campbell/The Journal of Marion Tebetts Banes.* Fayetteville, Arkansas: The Washington County Historical Society, 1977.

Wideman, Ruby Johnson, ed. *The Johnson Family: 1743-1978.* Portland, Or.: the author, 1978.

Williams, Betty. "Grandmother's House: A Personal History of the Walker-Knerr-Williams House," *Flashback,* publication of: the Washington County Historical Society, 33.3 (August 1983): 1-20: 33.4 (November 1983): 11-31.